A Room for Us

A Room for Us
Devan Burton

LITERARY PRESS
LAMAR UNIVERSITY

Copyright © Devan Burton 2021
All rights reserved

ISBN: 978-1-942956-88-4
Library of Congress Control Number: 2021939616

Cover Photo: ryypurnama
Editor: Paola Brinkley

Lamar University Literary Press
Beaumont, Texas

To the brokenhearted, the isolated, and the rejected—
The right word will change everything for us.

Recent Poetry from Lamar University Literary Press

Bobby Aldridge, *An Affair of the Stilled Heart*
Walter Bargen, *My Other Mother's Red Mercedes*
Charles Behlen, *Failing Heaven*
Jerry Bradley, *Collapsing into Possibility*
Mark Busby, *Through Our Times*
Julie Chappell, *Mad Habits of a Life*
Stan Crawford, *Resisting Gravity*
Glover Davis, *My Cap of Darkness*
William Virgil Davis, *The Bones Poems*
Jeffrey DeLotto, *Voices Writ in Sand*
Chris Ellery, *Elder Tree*
Dede Fox, *On Wings of Silence*
Alan Gann, *That's Entertainment*
Larry Griffin, *Cedar Plums*
Michelle Hartman, *Irony and Irrelevance*
Katherine Hoerth, *Goddess Wears Cowboy Boots*
Michael Jennings, *Crossings: A Record of Travel*
Gretchen Johnson, *A Trip Through Downer, Minnesota*
Ulf Kirchdorfer, *Hamlet in Exhile*
Jim McGarrah, *A Balancing Act*
J. Pittman McGehee, *Nod of Knowing*
Erin Murphy, *Ancilla*
John Milkereit, *Drive the World in a Taxicab*
Laurence Musgrove, *Bluebonnet Sutras*
Benjamin Myers, *Black Sunday*
Janice Northerns, *Some Electric Hum*
Godspower Oboido, *Wandering Feet on Pebbled Shores*
Carol Coffee Reposa, *Underground Musicians*
Jan Seale, *The Parkinson Poems*
Steven Schroeder, *the moon, not the finger, pointing*
Glen Sorestad, *Hazards of Eden*
Vincent Spina, *The Sumptuous Hills of Gulfport*
W.K. Stratton, *Betrayal Creek*
Wally Swist, *Invocation*
Ken Waldman, *Sports Page*
Loretta, Diane Walker, *Ode to My Mother's Voice*
Dan Williams, *Past Purgatory, a Distant Paradise*
Jonas Zdanys, *Three White Horses*

For information on these and other Lamar University Literary Press books go to www.Lamar.edu/literarypress

Acknowledgements

I am grateful to the editors of the following journals for publishing some of the poems collected in this book:

ALM Magazine
American Diversity Report
Door Is a Jar Magazine
Forth Magazine
Seshat Literary Magazine
Typishly Online

CONTENTS

Meditation: The Last Daffodil

15	In Celebration of Summer
16	In a State Park
17	What Rain Knows
18	That Which Does Not Stay at Home
19	When I Last Saw Water So Blue
20	Work, Without Faith
21	The Last Daffodil
22	Water
23	The Middle of October
24	Like Rain on a Sunday
25	Why Poets Write Poems about Falling Leaves
26	Clouds
27	Absence of Snow
28	Romance in the Social Media Age
29	When the Moon Blocked the Sun
30	All the Happiness
31	A Kitchen Window Is a Must
32	Rush Hour Traffic
33	Upheaval
34	It Takes Pressure to Make a Diamond
35	Finals
36	Road Trip
37	In the Morning
38	Intrusion
39	2 A.M. Wednesday
40	A Heartbeat in the Morning
41	First Morning
42	No Emoji
43	Vermont
46	Yaddo

Meditation: Tennessee Fancy

51	Langston Hughes, 2011
52	Creative Writing I
53	The Sleepover

54	Discarded
55	Twenty-Four Hour Chip
56	Alone with You
57	Overhearing a Conversation
58	Breakfast with Sarah
59	The Truth about Heroin
60	Changing a Shoelace at Thirty-Eight-Years Old
61	Stages
62	A Well-Traveled Wife
63	Tennessee Fancy
64	Post Grad Life
65	Down on My Luck
66	A Gentleman Only Knocks Twice
67	Prince Rogers Nelson
68	Thrift Store
69	If You Take a Picture of a Person, They'll Remember You Forever
70	One Hour on a Tuesday Morning
71	Sirens: April 19, 1995
72	Those Who Cannot
73	Terms and Conditions
74	Like Father, Like Son
75	The Myth of Frank Sinatra
76	My Mother's Longhand
77	High Culture
78	Off the Rack
79	Breakfast Poetry

Meditation: Black Lives in an Apple Orchard

83	To the White Children Playing Underneath My Apartment Window
84	Martin Luther King Jr. and Bull Connor Are Now Facebook Friends
85	Collective Bargaining with the Angels
86	Watching the Game
87	On Why Black History Month Is in February
88	Dual Enrollment
89	Sunday Afternoon on Minimum Wage
90	Public Service Announcement
91	Community College Student
92	Sharing the Crops
93	An Introduction to Literature Course
94	Take This Cup
96	Community College Instructor
97	Elegy for Trayvon

98	Teaching
99	Marvin Gaye and Liner Notes
99	Upstate, New York
101	Toni Morrison: In Airplane Mode
102	Black Lives in an Apple Orchard

Meditation: When Dreams Lose Their Grandeur

105	Mother-in-Law
106	A Nursing Home in Knoxville, Tennessee
107	When Dreams Lose Their Grandeur
108	Mother's Hour
109	I Want You Back
110	Parental Rights
111	Honor Thy Father
112	Long Term Memory
113	Driving West
114	In the Morning, He'll Be in Costa Rica
115	Passing Grandmother
116	Pep Rally for a Daughter

Meditation: The Last Daffodil

"Nature has been kind to us."

In Celebration of Summer

In the summer when my great-grandmother
kneeled in her garden,
she searched for answers.

She plucked the weeds away
from the heated earth
while sweat ran down her face.
The wide-brimmed straw hat
could not conceal
all of her hair—
sometimes white as the rare snowfall we witnessed,
sometimes white like the cotton her grandmother picked.
The steady rhythm established
when she poured a pail of water
over large tomatoes and virgin watermelons.

Often times she instructed me
on goodness and basketball
with the neighborhood children.
Instead,
in June's afternoon,
she asked me to sit with her
and handed me obnoxious growth to place in a white bag—
troublesome plants given to me from her aged green thumbs.

In a State Park

It is important to discard time—
the unit of measurement
that separates the living from the dead.
Here nature smells, and science is active.
Surrounding the aged-old geyser, the sulphur reigns.
The trees are kind enough
to shield wanderers from heat.
The trees are wise enough
to stand, and watch, and pray.
And the blue sky is pure.

What Rain Knows

The rain has a secret.
We know when she arrives.
The clouds applaud,
the sun hides,
and all the birds
fly
to the places
we pray to see.

Little drops
turn
into puddles.
The creeks and ponds,
they belong somewhere, too.

If we ask the rain,
she will be polite.
The lady will wait
until we're ready
for an answer.

That Which Does Not Stay at Home

The trees grew tall.
Then there was the sky,
blue with promises.
The blue sky of a New York summer
coincided with Tennessee.
The sun hid behind it all
and knew what I did not.
I waited for the light of the earth
to choose its fixed point.
I waited for the warmth of the earth
to look down upon us.
The sun looked blue too.
Light fell down upon me.
On the opposite page,
my shadow made a place for itself
while I wrote this.

When I Last Saw Water So Blue

for Karen

When I last saw water so blue,
was the dress she wore.
She knelt down to tend the garden
and convinced me I had a green thumb.
She was my great-grandmother.

When I last saw water so blue
was the dollar store baseball she threw.
She warned eight-year-old me,
the last pitch was coming.
And the hurled, manufactured plastic raced my way.
I forgot that my father was in prison.
She was my grandmother.

The blue of Northeast America was perfect.
The water lapped while it moved
alongside the bed and breakfast.

Work, Without Faith

Sore muscles
placed chipped cinder blocks
on July's ground.

I sat facing east—
wanting to be alone—
to revise my prayer.

Day and night
bonded
over low visible stars.

In the garden,
for the community,
small watermelons grew.

Like a newborn
connected to her mother,
summer's fruit was chained
to the busy earth,
and I waited for answered prayers.

I sat among the dew,
bell peppers,
and weeds.

The Last Daffodil

I drove by the last daffodil today.
In times recent,
small heaven-colored fixtures
paved the dull roadsides.
They danced with the wind.
They posed with Muslim children.
They cast their judgment
upon the drivers too busy
to stop and notice.
Yellow petals reflected the sun's health.
Tomorrow, the daffodils will disappear
because the earth overheats.
The ground from which they rose promise
me I will see daffodils next February.
I trust the earth.
May she keep global warming in his place.

Water

I do not remember harsh water.
The drops that fell on my face
from a baptism were kind.

The water we ran through
as children—
during summer's punishment,
the yellow hydrants
forgave us—
with cool nourishment.

And with this hurricane,
death unspeakable,
with mothers sitting on roofs
conversing with unseen winds:

Don't let my baby suffer long.

This water has a name.
I remember it in a pool,
kissing a woman
who permitted me to.
I remember it in a tub,
cleansing away the dirt.
The city's filth covered me.
I do not remember this water of condemnation.

The next hurricane, like autumn,
will appear with its colors:
gray,
black,
and the purple,
to further the darkness
we did not ask for.

I do not remember
when the water was harsh.

The Middle of October

The new stories each leaf tells.
With the wind,
the rain,
the sun,
foliage falls from trees.
For October,
life is kind,
(if only for seconds).
In months,
after summer,
it does not exhaust
to walk,
to sing,
to drink coffee
from old white cups.
Excitement
happens when hearts beat
without anxiety.

Like Rain on a Sunday

There is something about rain—
that when it falls—
on a Sunday afternoon,
causes people to slow down their lives.
When the clear deluge pours
down from sun sky,
the crowd remembers the miracles:
the son that comes back home
from Iraq without a scar—
an aunt that fights
to stay clean from meth—
the evening roast that is not cooked
until it is brick dry. Joni Mitchell sings
before California comes into view, and today
a couple waits for their cup to run over.
And before the father can explain
the significance of rain to his daughter,
it ceases with only damp city streets
to serve as a reminder.

Why Poets Write Poems about Falling Leaves

And the first leaves fall.
They slash, dash, and flip.
Silent scene stealers.
Call them brown because
the earth spins around.
Families race down crowded roads
to claim isolated beach land
and stand next to strangers.
Call the leaves orange because
fires can still rage within a fireplace.
A grandmother waits for dialysis.
She prides herself in avoiding
a lifetime of gin,
but her kidneys are failing her.
One soft September morning
my lover leaves.
She misses her daughter
who schools in Nashville.
She tells me to write today.
I sit on the car's hood
with borrowed pen,
age-stained journal,
and wait for the same leaves
to break away from limbs and branches.
I struggle to capture autumn
in my rearview mirror.
I drive away,
disturbing piles of leaves.
Call them red because
all conversations must end.

Clouds

Even the clouds know when to call it a day.
As the evening advances, these once proud beings
move slower and lower before giving way to the night.

Clouds like snowflakes move the way they see fit.
Does one catch clouds in May the same way
they catch snowflakes in December?

On the best evenings, the day's remaining blue
becomes soft and close enough to touch.
Should we take the time to log off

and step outside to ponder clouds?
Should we have the life that makes
one rich and needs fulfilled?

Absence of Snow

She misspelled ubiquitous in a suicide letter.
All the scenes appeared and her mind raced.
A class of graduate students judged her.

The snow, proof of God's age, left the town bare.
She waited for the dry mornings
because he would resurrect, then.
He, strong like a mule,
he, quiet like steel
made her heart flesh-like again.

When he crashed into a guardrail,
she saw dark skid marks on bright snow.
Everywhere, she wanted him everywhere.
He, bright like the red on cherries.
He, tender like Sunday evenings
was needed everywhere.
For a second she rolled over, reached
for a pen, and wrestled with grammar.
Her heart stopped before she reached the typewriter.

Romance in the Social Media Age

The pond stood before us,
a winter blanket of snow.
I moved your scarf
to cover exposed skin.

The children from the school
skipped, shouted, and sang.
They carried smartphones
and stole the pictures that belonged to us.

I worked three years for the engagement ring.
Rehearsed falling to one knee.
Marry me, we can buy a house.
We could not hear because of the livestream.

Youth was a liability.
Moments committed to digital format
to vanish in a day.
If we were alone,
you could have pondered
forever with me.

When the Moon Blocked the Sun

I sat before my mother.
Her face was a canvas
with other's compositions—
cracked lips, black, circled eyes.
I helped apply makeup—
a foundation to conceal
the experience from the other suitors.
I pulled the blinds up.
Rain stopped.
Sun poured in.
A newlywed couple stood next to my apartment.
They looked in the direction of the eclipse
after the temperature dropped.
The duo, fresh off the showroom floor,
did not know that they were young.
I shared my glasses with them
and was told that I was a kind Negro.
The husband removed the protective lenses
and glanced at the sky. The bride corrected her groom.
Look away from the sun, sweetie.
My daughter called to ask if I saw totality.
She asked me to talk to God for her stepfather
because plot is dirty and twisted.
He sat behind her
          as she asked me to take back my name.
                            Her name.
His health was failing.
My health was strong.
Instead of praying, I studied the stars.
I counted them until I created new numbers.
The first time we met
you were leaving Pigeon Forge, Tennessee.
Homer told me that Penelope waited
twenty years for Odysseus to return.
Love only promises to endure.
You sat with your legs on the couch like a teenager.
The gap between our knees fueled racing hearts.
We parted in the nervous morning.
The eclipse left because it belonged to the underworld.
The souls departed.
The angels grew tired of singing.
The world gave us an opportunity.
The world thought well of us.

All the Happiness

I
Blue is the color of God's eyes.
When I touch all that is blue,
I feel at one with him.

II
When people say unkind things
about the color blue
my heart races.
(I don't understand
how they can hate
our father so.)

III
When I am the most lost
is when I look to the sky
and see gray instead.
The obscenity lingers in view
like a mother eating her young.

IV
The blue returns soon.
The blue sky is limitless.
Blue heals the world again.

A Kitchen Window Is a Must

Birds stained the window.
For the space below,
lawyers held office hours.

Out in the world,
the narrative proceeded,
and the moon hung in the distance.

When two bodies walked around,
the apartment became a palace.
Enough warmth for the winter.

The end of September
inspired moments of reflection.
If the voices below only knew

the love that died
when obstacles became too hard.
The window in the kitchen.

Rush Hour Traffic

Before the child holds
her hand in the air to block the sun—
before the old man
praises heaven for another day,
this morning needs to make a decision.
Like choosing a dress before court,
a fourth of the day
deliberates on whether joy reigns
or sorrow multiples.
Until the morning articulates her agenda,
you and me wait
for eternity to reveal himself
in early morning weather reports.

Upheaval

I saw you this morning—
heading to service,
looking at the sky,
colors of blue, pink,
and white streaked
across my world.

I thought about saying
a prayer on your behalf,
but you said God
had died of a heart attack.
Jesus had his passion.
I did too.

You walked with me
underneath a thrift store umbrella
during fierce rain.
We stood in an empty Wendy's parking lot,
and you convinced me to take you home.
Together we melted in my bedroom
in an attempt to conceal frustrations.
Your grandfather was dying in Illinois.
Unreturned phone calls
replaced our laughter
from the nights we exhaled.
The silence dissolved the look we shared
when our kisses became more.
A slammed apartment door
disturbed the still mornings.

A card reader at Yellow Chrome
told me you'd return.
Our friends looked away to stare
at the new guy who tagged along
when we gathered for coffee hour at church.

It Takes Pressure To Make a Diamond

In Moose Pond,
a boy wandered away
to find beauty.
His family did not notice
his absence until
it was time for dinner.
The trees deeper in the woods adopted him,
gave him shelter like any father would.
The water next to the land
gave him as much nourishment
as a mother could.
The light from the sun bared down.
No rainbows, unicorns, or parables
brought him back.
A boy named diamond did not shine,
and nature consumed him.
The untamed, untouched elements pondered,
then kept him for pressure.

Finals

I remember when we slept in after sunrise,
that inviolable time when the night shielded us
from the day and reminders of obligations.
The teakettle purred while you suspended your consciousness.
We ignored deadlines for semester research papers.
A light steam rose in the kitchen,
and the water rumbled
like children running in streets in June.

I did not ask what dreams you lived through while you slept.
Either you'd tell me a lie
or say something that had little logic.
I knew you belonged to someone else.
His name in permanent blackness was visible.
Textbooks, rulers, and name badges looked like jealous lovers
the night I picked you up. Your daughter was with her father,
and you wanted to feel young again.

Road Trip

I work because I owe.
Work tries to own me.
Underneath the gray clouds, we address the past.
There is a difference between blue and gray.

If the clouds fell from the sky,
the landing would harm us.
Flying pieces,
lingering smoke,
but then there is the blue sky.

You see the blue
and you live again.
On my way
I think about my family.

In Virginia,
the leaves are falling too.
The difference between the gray sky, the blue sky,
is the difference between the past and future.

In the Morning

No one looks out for me anymore.
The budget handed to me
because of my salary
makes life crucial.

In the morning,
quiet voices of responsibility
sends a chill over my body.
I wake and my feet dangle off the side of the bed.

At 5:17, two garbage men place the discarded items of our lives
in the back of their truck.
I miss my childhood,
when the answers I debated were doled out.

It is my fault.
I did not leave a trail to follow back to my youth.
When sitting at the kitchen table,
I think about being a child
and ponder why the rush.

Intrusion

You never thought of geology as a real science,
but you entered the cave
at Tipton Haynes Historic site.
Returning to daylight,
you wiped the dirt on your knees away
with the back of your hands
and led me past the tall grass.
Stumbling over my untied shoe laces,
I found myself face first in God's ground
that damp September morning.
A faint breeze revealed the smell of onions.
You painted at my place while I showered.
You held me when I was clean again.

The next summer, I walked to the nearest grocery store.
You stood in frozen foods
with your new boyfriend.
When his dirt-caked five o' clock shadow
graced the top of the head I kissed,
emotions meddled.
With closed eyes, I placed a white onion
under my nose and saw you twice:
passing by the bedroom
while you slept in my t-shirt after a late dinner,
the day you walked near me
on our college campus
head hung low in a failed attempt
to avoid the fall's first raindrops.

Tipton Haynes closed for the winter.
Looking in the direction of the onions,
left of the lowering sun,
I could not smell them.
I stood among tomatoes and grapes
in a health food store when a woman
in a wheelchair asked me to hand her a pair
of white onions which she pressed to her face.

2 A.M. Wednesday

When I can no longer call
for rain to fall upon the fires
in the forest, I remember the clouds.
Where we stood,
we pointed to them
and approved their movement
like their purpose was to entertain us.
I forgot our dialogue
in my quiet hours, and I spoke for you
in my time of need.
Life should be more
than overdrawn bank accounts
and raising gas prices.
I remember the sound of rain—
first, tender then forceful
as it made its way from the land
of the unseen
to the hearts that race
from one morning to the other.

A Heartbeat in the Morning

for Mary Oliver

When I wake each morning,
I leave heaven behind.
The sounds and sights appear
like each town I have driven
away from, watching the landscape
fade in a rearview mirror.
I stand before a window
and watch a proud cardinal attach
himself to a tree branch
and move his head, side to side,
and I count each blink
of his ebony eyes. Perhaps
he is trying to remember
God's face too.
Each morning,
light runs
across the sky.
Such a canvas
to watch artwork.
Such a day
to spend seconds,
ticking steady
like a heartbeat.

First Morning

I want to see the morning again—
with all of its colors and sounds.
Shapeless, darkness comprehends
soft white and bold blue.
The morning calls into mind
that truth is real,
and seen with the naked eye.
I want to say that my mother
saw such a morning in her life.
Before she stole new drinks
from old bottles.
In the morning,
filled with possibilities
like leaves in May,
full, rich, numerous.
I want to see the morning again.
And hear the sounds of yesterday
as they creep closer to rivers
and creeks among the other creatures
in nature.

No Emoji

And we walked away from the pond.
The smell of rain was clear.
Along with the gray clouds,
the grass was receptive.

I realized you were new to love.
Like trying to explain the moon,
I lost the words
I needed to close the deal.

You realized I was new to love,
and language betrayed you.
There were not enough words.
There were no right words.

We made it.
Gentle taps of rain at first
became muted downpour later.
In my car, our hands merged, because we made it.

Vermont

I. Sunlight in Vermont

does not poke the face,
like in Alabama,
does not press herself
against the body,
like in Tennessee.
The light of the earth suggests
summer is with us. And the people walk
two by two, remembering the game of catch
with their departed fathers.
The pond in Manchester does not move
with the human respiratory system.
Sunlight in Vermont is green, yellow,
and black underneath porch umbrellas
at restaurants where the soup of the day
is chicken vegetable.

II. When the Wind Blows in Vermont

a neighbor talks to me.
He inquires about the children,
the level of my blood pressure,
and if I know the difference between a no-hitter and a perfect game.
The wind does not carry the weight of history
like it does in Washington D.C.
The bushes shake—
polite as a handshake,
kind like a mother pointing me the way home.
Clouds are not broken,
and the God I believe in goes fishing.

III. The Children Would Not Fit in the Car

My son counts the stop lights,
the youngest daughter points out
that Vermont is not New York City,
and the firstborn finds a place
to speak with Jesus Christ (if the children were with me). Vermont—
once only a place on a map—exists, questions, and stares.
The Depression era stores have not aged with time,
nor does brown grass grow underneath bare windows.
(802) fits in my pocket.
A timber-truss covered bridge connects.

Yaddo

I
Poetry has always been open to me.
All I've ever really needed:
a pen and a pad,
and I translate the unspoken to the words which men speak.
I turn to free verse like a woman who has the right to choose.
I look for line breaks when life breaks me.
When I sit in front of Yaddo,
I understand why everything is not poetry.

II
A saint from Georgia also sits at the grounds.
In Iowa, she writes down her questions
because the professors comprehend her not.
A few short stories later, Flannery labors away at a novel.
Her wise blood confuses us.
She does not hold our hands.
All the answers reside upon the pages.
In the rose garden, the fragrance tickles her nose.
The other residents sit with her and laugh with her.
The obedient Catholic studies
the differences between the North and South.
A young priest administers to her last rites.
She waves him away because she has revisions to make.

III
A gay man removes his shoes
and morning dew embraces his feet.
He leaves Harlem behind;
he ignores his father who measures him less.
A preacher's son, he writes about race.
He believes white people
who practice racism are sick like polio patients.
He adds words to history as the cure.
Baldwin thinks about the fire next time;
his heart beats in a city where nobody knows his name;
he laments his sweet Lorraine.
At 413 Broadway, James does not hear the word coon,
even as a jazz trio plays "Fly Me to the Moon."

IV
I attended East Tennessee State University.
My teachers comprehended not
why a black man wanted to study literature.
They believed I was better suited for sports management or music.
My poems celebrated not their politics, mountains, or heritage.
I was told that I could not sit next to another student of color
because we were not in Detroit.
In the end, I wrote a former instructor a letter.
It took him a year to respond—
in that time, I taught students who would earn more than me.
I watched first generation scholars grow—
the content of his letter filled a post card.

V
He comes from across an ocean.
The ladies melt when he speaks.
In the weeks of late May,
he suffers because the daffodils are gone.
He walks in the garden.
The next volume of poetry is due, and he has not seen a hawk in months.
He was born to write poetry.
All of life could fit on the pages.
He smiles because a young woman stares at him.
Ted Hughes has nothing to confess in a world of writers whose lives
are an open book.
His eyes now are June morning bright because he sees a deer in the distance.
The doe nibbles on a rose.
The poet takes to pen and pad.

VI
Her father is a teacher.
He dies while she is still young.
She is bright enough to perceive
that happy endings are only written.
Plath calls her father a bastard, once.
Such power such freedom such darkness the word creates.
She lives under a code.
Poetry is to be quaint, rustic, and polite.
In a hospital, after the birth of a son, she is sick.
The voices tell her to die.
She listens to them.
Before the gas stove in the kitchen overpowers her,

before her husband burns her manuscript,
she stands on the land the Trasks left behind.
Sylvia thinks about how one measures 400 acres.

VII
Langston Hughes stands next to me.
He should be a ghost, faint, and white.
But he is close enough that I smell jazz.
In a voice,
part admirer,
part jealous,
part father-like,
he tells me to write.
He does not win the Pulitzer,
but high school students read his lyrical lines for ages.
I stand at Yaddo on a Saturday morning.
Signs inform me that the area is private.
Before now, poetry was never a crime, nor off limits to me.
If everyone writes poetry, poetry will change everything.

VIII
I look once more and Langston Hughes is gone.
Flannery O' Connor,
James Baldwin,
Ted Hughes,
Sylvia Plath
are part of the artist colony.
Once again I am home, standing in a classroom,
thinking about Yaddo without interruption.
When I face a student who challenges me
when I say literature is important,
I will remember the barriers of the upstate New York property.
Then the moment when my soul
and the souls of writers departed are one in the same.

Meditation: Tennessee Fancy

"If circumstances and situations should conspire against us."

Langston Hughes, 2011

In Harlem,
July presses
her face against the earth.
I carry raisins I bought
from Walgreens while travelling
through Greenwich Village.
The sun is lazy.
Silver clouds, gray clouds, black clouds,
frolic across the sky.
Manhattan
did not
talk to me.

On the corner of 125th Street
and Lennox Avenue, a woman
with rust-stained shopping carts
asks me about my mother.
When third afternoon light appears,
I crush the small red box,
and wrinkled grapes
fall
on scorching sidewalk.

Creative Writing I

for Richard Wilbur

When you had already written volumes,
I shared my poetry with you.
You wrote more than I did
on my best submissions.
Comments in blank verse
crowded out my metaphors.
Do not be clever.
I was a transfer student
from a community college
desperate for greatness,
but you instructed me
to look for what was unwritten.

I sit in your departure tonight.
Your verses litter the universe.
I long to write a line someday
that Wordsworth would have wished for.
I don't work with muses anymore
(they are too demanding).

The Sleepover

I love the way my girlfriend smells in the morning.
While she lies next to me, her hair covers the pillow
like snow covers the ground.
She lifts an arm in the air
and when the temperature is just right
she dives into the day.

I'm still learning what her faces mean,
and when I confuse them she smiles.
Maybe she's not ready for heavier matters.
I will not tell her about the extra key
to my place I had made
or ask her thoughts
about white picket fences and taxes.
The three words I want to shout to the world
I'll whisper to her as she sleeps.

She has a toothbrush above the sink,
milk in the fridge,
and reading glasses on the coffee table.
When I head outside to start my car
in February's terse, cold morning
she locks the bathroom door before she showers.
When I see her again,
the walls will not matter.
When I see her again,
all of my bricks will fall.

Discarded

Weren't we lovers once?
The couple who laughed at tired jokes,
braved the ice-glazed roads for refried beans,
and sat in an empty campus parking lot waiting
for answers.
I never judged your idiosyncratic breath,
asked you to wash the dishes,
or sit through my revisions.
You wanted to heal the heart
one hypothesis at a time
and lifted mine away to your lab.
Nicking DNA pulled
you away, and I was discarded
along with your off-yellow dress,
dorm room fridge, and the maple coffee table
that I carried for you—
the one that bruised my left knee.
No reminder for you that I had been there.
No reminder that you let me in.

Twenty-Four Hour Chip

I sit in an AA meeting.
Tony attends because of his daddy issues.
Mary because she cuts herself.
I'm here because I drink like the leaves fall in October.

When you were mine,
we drank to forget our low-paying jobs
at your mother's diner,
where you were groped
and I was called a coon.
At my place, Sam Cooke sang
about Saturday nights and iceboxes.
Nothing warmed me like when you danced.
When you left,
I drank because I wanted you—
because I found your socks in my laundry.

Bob cries when he talks
about the partner he lost in May.
At meeting's end,
Samantha hands out chips.
Mary accepts a green one.
Tony receives the blue.
I take a twenty-four-hour chip for today
and steal one for the morning.

Alone with You

You and I came home
underneath my brown jacket
because the warm November rain
would cause your face to run.

On a table, before us,
a chipped glass
and oval ice cubes sat.
You sulked on the couch
because where we were heading
you had been there before.

You towered on the table.
I praised your contents.
Brown.
Distilled.
Aged.
Removing your top
made me feel like a teenager,
dizzy with possibilities before each kiss.
Some call you bourbon.
I call you
when I'm down.
I call you
when I ache.
When I'm alone with you,
I pray that God loses my address.

Overhearing a Conversation

for e.e.

The day before the scheduled ultrasound
she waits to hear a heartbeat.
The pregnancy test was not
enough of a confirmation for her—
she expects the cold gel
to fall on her warm skin.
She prepares herself for the press
of the firm wand against her yielding stomach.
What if there's no heartbeat?
She wants life to grow inside her
because her father missed too many birthdays,
because it never snowed enough
in Wisconsin when she was young,
because she felt alone in Europe.
Before she falls asleep,
she talks to God, again.
She prays for a successful nine months,
and settles for grace if science delays her dream.

Breakfast with Sarah

Before the kitchen light fell asleep on the bedroom floor
she arrived after another break up.

Her latest boyfriend left her, the boyfriend before him cheated,
and the one before him liked men.

I changed the bedsheets in my room, lay on the couch,
then watched as she walked to the bedroom and slammed the door.

After the sun rose, muffins baked in the oven,
eggs cooked on the stove, and Sarah stood in the hallway.

My wrinkled t-shirt and faded sweatpants covered her
like curtains a bare window. With black-cornered ham sizzling,

she sat at the kitchen table with an empty cup, talking.
I don't want much.

Her wild blue eyes rested tame in the morning.
Her breath cooled the kitchen.

She judged the decaf coffee I served,
drinking it like water.

The Truth about Heroin

When we walked together
—hand in hand—
she asked me about the man
sitting among the new daffodils.
Clouds covered his true green eyes
when he asked for money.
His amber hair was a 12 year old's mess.
He exposed
his bare feet in the March cold
like walking on the ocean's edge.
His four asphalt black toes
crashed against the other six white ones.
Syringe appeared
but the vial concealed.
No lid for the needle,
no need for conversation.
He told us to enjoy our day
and we passed him heading back to my loft.

Changing a Shoelace at Thirty-Eight-Years Old

When I gave it a tug,
I noticed the age.
Black—
thin—
a relic—
elastic.

The shoelace unraveled
step by step
with worn aglets.
And the candle wicks
burned once too often.

I replaced the shoelace
on a Friday morning.
Tips fed through eight eyelets.
Had I pulled myself up
by one of them
we both would have snapped.

Stages

for Ara

What? No. When? How? Sweet Christ.
The iron unplugged, the cat fed,
and the front door locked. I can fend
for myself. Can't I?
Goddamn it.
If one more jerk cuts me off!
Don't you get it? I need to see her.
Maybe she's still breathing.
Maybe she's still waiting, for me.
I was unaware of my speed.
The registration is underneath
the insurance, officer. I will be careful,
thanks.
You are cold and dark.
As quiet as my frost-kissed windshield in late January.
You were never the praying
kind because you thought of prayer
as a hassle.

A Well-Traveled Wife

Her marriage is a flat tire at dawn.
She'll wait until there's enough light for a change.

The small town apartment she shares with her roommates
is not the Virginia acre she shared with her husband.
From eight to four and four to ten she works for the tips
the customers leave her in a roadside diner.
Resting in warm bath water at night,
she ponders while her family falters.

She'd exchange all the twilights on a beach
for another wedding night,
for another ceremony,
one where her father was sober
just long enough for a last walk.

Quiet irrigation floods her field. It starts
above her nose, races down her cheeks,
then off her chin, descending to the hips
that are not touched.

Tennessee Fancy

I watch for the leaves to fall
shop for dirty typewriters
drink coffee in the morning
read poetry before the sunrise
wave at the police officers I pass
work with students younger than my children
think about graduate school when facing pressure at work
wait for class to start
standing in an east Tennessee hallway,
living.

Post Grad Life

We were not made for Yale.
A.C.T. and S.A.T. scores revealed to others what we knew.
College is meant for students with textbook histories.
Your father owed a debt to Georgia, Alabama, and Arkansas.
Perhaps there was a link between my stuttering
and my mother's cocaine-laced post nasal drip.
Year after year the acceptance letters divided
the goats from the sheep.

You were obsessed with Rhode Island.
The university served their sweet tea with three packets of sugar.
When you moved north, you made trails for yourself
back home to remember later. My mother started rehab in the fall,
again.
Same tears.
Same bruised knuckles.
Same list of men who wrote her epilogue stood in the background.
A community college would take me because they needed
an extra pair of hands on the ground crew.

You were obsessed with Rhode Island.
Scholarships fitted you like necklaces.
With all the revisions attempted, and nights spent sitting
at library tables, your brown eyes would never turn blue.
I helped your father with a job application.
He found success until he placed a letter in his social security number.
Embarrassed, he robbed a bank.

The August night before you left to attend college convocations,
dance at the sorority balls,
and drive to Maine on quiet autumn days, I asked for a kiss.
You told me I was only a friend.
Someone to cry with when talking trust funds judged your wardrobe.
Someone to avoid when you came home for summer visits.
Last winter, I sent you a wedding invitation.
Your sister wanted to know if you were a plus one.

Down on My Luck

If I sat in a wheelchair
because life was unkind
I would want someone to push me.

If I lost my sight
because life was unkind
a pure soul must stand next to me

and describe the sunrise
in metaphors that would heal my soul.

If I stood behind a cash register
because life was unkind
bagging groceries at minimum wage

I would expect that customer to look me
in my eyes and call me sir.

Love conquers hate.
Dignity restores the spirit
when fate's heavy hands steal from us.

A Gentleman Only Knocks Twice

Lady,
I want your face
to imprint on my pillow.
Long hair,
short hair,
I don't care.
Lady,
I want to see you
in the morning light,
when all is right
and simple concerns
have melted away.
Lady,
I'll leave you alone,
now. All we share
is a stare. When you look
at me, I ponder about
heaven and faithfulness.
If I see you again,
I'll work up enough hubris
to praise your taste in shoes.

Prince Rogers Nelson

My daughter is old enough to ask where I have been.
Perhaps she is old enough to understand how debt
can cripple a person. Maybe someday she will discover
that when her stepfather presses a slice of birthday
cake into her face tiny, tornadoes form in my chest.
Maybe someday she will learn that I wait for her
to hang up first after each phone call.
Maybe someday I will hear a dove cry.

The night my mother died alone in Oklahoma
I stood on an empty soccer field.
I fell to my knees and remembered rain.
My mother, alive.
Laughing,
Dancing,
Black.
The purple dress she wore
clung to her hips before I turned away.
I left the grass and stars,
a motherless child born new to the world.

Thrift Store

I walked around the thrift store
like it was a museum, looking at the details
of yesterday, one footstool at a time.
I passed posters of the World War II era,
the ones in which Uncle Sam stared at me.
The leisure suits as brown as new spring dirt.
I found albums that completed someone's Saturday night:
flipped through Al Hirt,
Peter, Paul and Mary,
James Taylor, and Ray Charles.
Some albums possessed nicks that caught my fingernail.
Some records looked as new as November mornings.
America's soundtrack collected dust next
to discarded *Life* magazines.

If You Take a Picture of a Person, They'll Remember You Forever

for Jack

She wants to touch the water.
Live forever with less gray in her hair.
I do not know her,
but I instruct the elementary school teacher,
from behind a Nikon,
to stand straight.
I tell her she is as pretty as a picture
and her smile appears without prompting.
She gathers coastal living magazines when her husband joins us.

The mechanic stands wherever she tells him to.
For a moment they are young.
He removes his baseball cap.
I can see their wedding day.
This can be your Christmas card.

She moves closer to the reflection,
of sky and clouds,
inserts her toes,
and becomes one with the water.

One Hour on a Tuesday Morning

He remembers his former classmates:
The redhead he had a crush on,
The jock who pissed in his shoes during gym class,
The best friend who was gay.
Sitting in a small office on a Tuesday morning,
a therapist asks him to think about a time—
the days before the deaths,
before responsibilities.
He thinks about his friends—
the ones who chose death in the early, quiet mornings.
The suicides held forth their hands
and whispered to each of them.
In a car, a kitchen, a shower.
The suicides had whispered to him, too.
What would you tell thirteen-year-old you?
No such thing as a stupid question.
He watches the clock like a video.
The minutes are imposing figures. Bullies.
While scheduling his next appointment,
he remembers his former classmates,
the ones who answered when suicide called.

Sirens: April 19, 1995

She saw souls leaving the earth that day.
In a studio apartment with her husband she felt
cacophonous waves as they rippled below on the city streets.
Heat like hell consumed the cool April morning.
The week before, her birthday, she celebrated
her age with water-laced bourbon, scratched Johnny Cash records,
and torn photos of her sons back east.
Glass replaced the air.
Silence was louder than five o' clock traffic.
When she stood on the sidewalks, McVeigh's fire burned her toes.
Sirens blared even late at night.
Sirens blared even years later.
Before the reflection pool.
Before the chairs were placed on the well-kept lawn.
All there were that climbed to the sky were souls.
The father who drank too much.
The grandmother who tended to her daughter's children.
The son who skipped school, again.
Kind spirits, corrupted constitutions, rising,
leaving work undone.

Those Who Cannot

And the smoke disappears above us.
In a small room.
One window for life's narrative to unfold.
It's not happening.
She holds my poems in one hand,
and ashes from her cigarette falls to the floor.
I ask for clarification.
She speaks in German, French, and Latin.
(If she is using metaphors, the meanings are lost on me.)
Pictures of Poe, Longfellow, and Dickinson offer support.
She sits before me,
and shares rebuke after rebuke.
She teaches poetry,
but does not write it herself.

Terms and Conditions

When I said it was just a kiss,
you ought to have believed me.

We sat at the table—
each night—for dinner.

It rained that night.
We thought the clouds concealed us.

She and I caught the same train.
Once we were strangers.

I did not have to be told twice.
The dishes piled in the sink

were washed when we finished our meal.
I broke bread with you.

We reclaimed our identities.
The embrace ended.

I should have told her,
I had a wife at home.

Like Father, Like Son

I will reside
among the dark sky,
cool wind, and unforgiving earth.
It rained the day my father met the stars.
The clouds kept all the beauty of the world away.
And the fire did too.
Men seized him from a trial,
moved him through the city streets like cattle.
The end result:
he hung from an oak tree,
his neck curved like the letter "L,"
sable hands close together, like he was praying.
I am not praying.
I do not seek to disturb God.
Children, with their father's blond hair,
placed my lifeless body
on a truck bed.
Let him wade in the water.
Tonight, I will be one with the stars.

The Myth of Frank Sinatra

Every man thinks they're Frank Sinatra
when the moon is close enough.
We raise our hands
as if
the light flourishes
because we snap our fingers.

With our close friends
we answer to Francis,
and the music is sharp—
ice cubes clinking
in a small glass of whiskey,
dignified for Sunday night,
sustainable for Wednesday evening,
bold and intoxicating,
like sailors on shore leave.

The Hoboken poet scats his way to Las Vegas,
and again we think of the moon,
witchcraft, and the gender of luck.
With a black fedora crooked on the head,
we hum a tune,
pondering the amount of string it takes to hold the world.

My Mother's Longhand

I could not put you in a basket
like was done for Moses. I drove
away because I was a flame. Nature
showed me that I could not provide.
My mother would raise you.
She kept you away from the streets.
When I left you, I slept on crowded streets
in the functioning car we rode around in.
I drove to Florida, Nebraska, California,
but made my home in Oklahoma.
I tried to forget about the tears
you shed when I called you collect from a phone booth.
I ran to an old phone booth
to hide from frigid rain
and jealous lovers. Life in Knoxville
had to be simple for you.
You learned the English alphabet
has twenty-six letters and a history.
The thing to understand about history
is that anyone can write it.
As a mother I understood
the dynamics of life.
I felt the knife's cold blade
against my swollen neck.
If I saw you again, I'd kiss your neck,
discuss the weight you gained, the children
you begat, and the life you made because
I drove away. Instead, you came to Oklahoma
in an oil-leaking car to carry
my ashes back to Tennessee.
You brought me to Tennessee,
adorned with a ring, in a basket.
Together, we wrote history.

High Culture

The Holocaust museum birthed poetry
among the relics, icons, and smells.
Jewish verses,
Jewish voices,
shared with me
what people did not listen to.
Poets who wrestled with demons
thought enough of future students
to jot down a few words.
In their lyrics,
trees stood like judges
waiting to cast down their decisions.
Poetry is the work
people must do
to articulate the unspoken.
Tears ran down my face
because the downtrodden
spoke in meter with imagery.
Textbooks cannot replace—capture—
the sound of fear.
Poetry possesses the life
to connect us to hate
and redemption.

Off the Rack

In your shirt,
the heart regulates
the flow of blood (and who you love).
The soft blend,
white years ago—
has met time:
ink pen marks,
coffee stains,
crumbs from a bagel.
The bills to pay causes you
to roll the arm sleeves tight.
Life has a direction.

Morning produces a first light—
dim, even as it spills across the kitchen floor.
The shirt in the closet
hangs—
waiting to experience
proof of life.

Breakfast Poetry

Let us have breakfast
while the receding darkness
comes to terms with its function.
The coffee brews,
the light shines from the ceiling,
and the traffic clocks in.

This breakfast is not extraordinary.
Man has the meal every morning.
Woman thinks about the eggs
before the rest of the family.
Let us have breakfast,
because it is the right thing to do.

The blessed fast
we break
because we can.
Toast and tea.
You and me.
A table scattered with poetry.

Meditation: Black Lives in an Apple Orchard

"The political climate is different for us."

To the White Children Playing Underneath My Apartment Window

for Gwendolyn Brooks

You own the world.
And run about the land
as though you named
the animals. Your mother's
voice floats into my kitchen.
It is Sunday, and the pastor
called you good. When you ride
around be aware of what you see.
Life is privileged behind tinted windows.
                    The college
you want to attend will not think
twice about admitting you.
The neighborhood you move
into will praise your sons
and open their country club.
Your father will return home
after a police officer issues
him a ticket for speeding.
You who skip and flip beneath
my apartment window. Take stock
of the skin you are living in.
Your charmed life waits.

Martin Luther King Jr. and Bull Connor Are Now Facebook Friends

Martin logs in,
studies humanity,
and ponders deleting his account.
Before service he looks for Connor's wall.
Two hundred and thirty-eight people like a picture he shares:
a young man,
hanging from a poplar tree,
dried blood stains his Sunday's best.
Early daffodils bloom.
The politician is in the photo too.
He stands among the other men in the crowd.
On April 4, 1968, the negro minister adds more to his dream.
Best day ever. Hashtag.
He steps outside onto a Memphis hotel balcony and meets eternity.
The elder statesman searches the preacher's wall
and reposts his composition.

Collective Bargaining with the Angels

I sat across the small table
from an ex-Army ranger
looking into his coffee cup.

*Boy, when I lived in Kuwait,
I ate like a king, boy.*
Our orders arrived,
he ate from his plate and then mine.
The butter on the waffles were just enough.

We parted ways and he stood
next to the interstate exit
with his torn, misspelled sign.

Homeless veterans scatter American streets—
blessed leaves falling
from imposing trees underneath
the admonishing sky—
the angels have stopped fighting for us.

Watching the Game

for James P.

America for me
is having black conversations
with white friends.
When asked
why million-dollar football players
kneel
I thought of
Tamir,
Michael,
and the Minnesota gentleman
who had as much right to carry a gun
as he did to drive.
I cannot see
the soldiers my friend
—the medic in Iraq—tried
to save.
I do not know the sound the flag
made when it fell upon each coffin.

Some scars are visible.
Most scars are not visible.

The following week,
we studied defensive schemes
towns apart.

On Why Black History Month Is in February

When old man Moses
could no longer see farther
he thought of freedom.
The babies and the wife
did not register until
the chains caused his ankles to ache.
He heard the tales and myths
of the other figures
like Douglass, Equiano, and Tubman.
The shackles grew tighter and smaller
as he moved. *Live chained,*
die free.
He sat on Tennessee stump
and meditated on Israel's Moses.
How he lived in forty years wilderness.
The slave raised his criminal arms
and saw
iron and sunshine.

Dual Enrollment

When I email my boss,
I think about the choice of words—
and my college professor.
We gave him hell that fall.
Susan blamed him for her first F. Jeremy created
a noose he never placed on the instructor's car.
Ashley flirted always. I watched to see if he
stood for the pledge of allegiance.
I did not tell him
he was my favorite black teacher
(he was the only black teacher we ever had).
When we gave a wrong answer
his octave rose as he said *interesting*.
He failed in law school,
but often he spoke of due diligence.
The best dresser—
he did not wear t-shirts and jeans—like
the other teachers.
The cursor on the screen blinks.
Behind it I see him tapping his dull pencil
on my composition in our high school's library.
He struggles to communicate.
I see my college professor's yellow tie
as clear as a bright October morning.

Sunday Afternoon on Minimum Wage

After she throws away her cigarette
she picks grass from the ground.
In her moment of freedom
she looks at the different blades
as if it was the first time.
She does not pay attention
to the traffic at the end of
the convenient store's parking lot.
Perhaps she picked the same grass
when she was younger
before the veil that separated
her and womanhood ripped in two.
She lifts her hand to her face and blows.
The grass that fuels her imagination
dances with the air
while it falls to the ground.
For a second, life is grand.
She forgets that she works
for minimum wage on a Sunday
and listens to customers as they call
her baby, honey, and sugar.

Public Service Announcement

The parent stood before the counter
at the bookstore with her
children running around. She did
not care about the thunder
her sons made while crashing
into each other. The crescent-
shaped bruise she wore
dimmed her bright green eyes.
I fell from a tree, today.
Her laughter was off key
and she looked over her
shoulders like a stranger
in a new town. She took
her order to a table and sat with her
twins. The mother listened
to them praising their father while
her lips trembled.

Community College Student

She did not know what to do with me.
Like I was the parent of one of her students.

It was August and the assignments were relentless.
The youth sneered.

The professor erased the content.
Class was completed and she approached me.

After all of these years.

I borrowed $15
to submit an application

to a community college.
In the mornings, I stood in the back of class.

I worked a double shift the night before.
Dumping grease traps, writing thesis statements.

A month of saved overtime pay bought textbooks during midterm week.

Sharing the Crops

Daddy would receive more lashes,
if all the strawberries were not picked,
by sundown.
Sister and I
tried to pick with speed,
but the berries broke in our hands.
In the distance,
other families sang
to a quiet god.
The strawberries stood in a basket.
I could not tell if the crimson stains
on our daddy's hands came from the fruit,
or if it was blood again.
Mama sought for Jesus when the owner appeared.
Daddy asked to speak to his boss away from us.
Hot August tears ran down Mama's face
when the first clap lingered in the air.

An Introduction to Literature Course

I believe Jesus was a poet.
When he sat
before the woman caught
in the act of adultery,
and ran his bare fingers
in the dirt,
he wrote a poem.
Life hands us lyrics.
Sometimes the lines rhyme.
Sometimes the lines are free.
If I express what is on my heart,
you will cover your ears
like I'm singing off-key.
Jesus thought of another line to add to the stanza.
And the used typewriter that sailed
along the coastline of Vietnam traveled to me
on the back of a UPS truck.
Tell me why we must seek for normal.
Tell me why we must hate what we do not understand.
Jesus did not consult spellcheck.

Take This Cup

I
I can see clean and clear now
though the rain is still here.
But it will be gone soon.
The light drizzle
will make the grass sparkle
when the sun appears.
Tradition says Christ rose on a day like this.
Did he want to drink too?
Be clear my vision.
I can see the road that brought me here.

II
Where were you yesterday, Daddy?
I was sick.
Mama told Aunt Meme you were drunk.
And the six year old brings me to my knees.
I should leave the brown hell that separates me
from my princess, my namesake, and my growing rose.
Hello, my name is Lee, and I'm an alcoholic.
Hi, Lee.

III
I'm back at Joe's and the bartender is too busy to talk.
In times past, he gave me bourbon on the rocks
and the drink felt more like a bomb than a shot.
I don't come here often, I come here a lot.
Deacon Tim tells me that hell will have brimstone and fire,
then leaves with his gin and tonic and sits three seats away
to watch the Red Sox and Yankees play.
If this glass of whiskey is an apple
then let me take a bite.

IV
I am waiting for my reflection to become beautiful again.
Behind the somber morning's mist,
the day's first light reveals that the city
is drowsy and dilatory.
The quiet steam, which rises from my coffee cup,
reminds me of what I have lost,
and what remains.

What should I do with this time?
I mean, what should we do with this time?

Community College Instructor

I celebrated the birth of his son.
Instructor and student were equal.
His girlfriend slept in their truck
while he attended the evening Intro to Sociology class.
All of September consumed him.
Cleaning carpets.
Baking potatoes.
And the offspring slept at home.
The absences took their toll.
He stood before me,
tears formed like a child:
Am I failing?
In the emotion,
I saw a picture that was whole.
I saw a picture that was ripped.
The difference was the lack of interruption.
In later autumns,
he passes a community college.
His friends laugh and ride in the truck bed.

Elegy for Trayvon

Hoodies frighten me now.
Green white and gray made
with cotton blend to keep
the world away. The hood concealed
your head from the weather.
On certain days, black earbuds infused
your stubborn disposition with the words
of Biggie, Lefteye, and Tupac.
On the rough days, the elements
would not leave you alone.
The cotton thread blend shielded
you from February's chill.
Only if bullets could be so cold.

Teaching

I teach a son of a klansman.
Somedays I am a black man.
Somedays I am an assistant professor of English.
Behind the blond hair
that falls over his blue eyes,
the white board looms large.
He cannot spell.
His late submissions are half attempts
at the scholarship his family laughs
at over Sunday dinners.

Is it hard being a black teacher?

I know the answer
like I know the number
of clouds in the sky.
On the good days,
he shakes my hand
and we make eye contact.
I teach in the 21st century.
The days where I can stand
and lecture do not compute with YouTube clips.
When he calls me boy,
he covers with the term sir.
Loud like thunder,
tender like new-birthed cows.

He is rural,

and I delete my daily lesson plans.
He tells me he wants to follow in his father's footsteps.
Work in the garage, change tires, and vote conservative.

You my first colored teacher.

I ask him to place the teacher before the color.
He does not understand.
I still do not have an answer for his question.

Marvin Gaye and Liner Notes

for Allen Ginsberg

The short arm held firm as the stylus fell.
Black vinyl birthed a groove.
With magic, black was given a sound.
Morning fog and silence hovered until quizzical men greeted each other.
A saxophone blared and a gentle mist appeared.

Forty years later, I can talk about loss:
watched a great-grandmother lose her mind
after she defeated Jim Crow. She did not
want to remember using a separate bathroom
from her white students; my grandmother was as smart
as her German and Irish colleagues, but she could not vote,
nor could she refrain from drinking the cheap champagne
that tickled her negro brain.
And the record spun.

The bassline checked in with me, waiting for confirmation,
my decision to remain black. All the voices of humanity
were found in track after track.
The record became a world.
Each song was a different season of the year.
The gentle mist—tears articulating rage—remained
while thinking about God.

If I am made in his image, would white supremacists hate him too?
It was Monday morning, and a chant of mercy filled my living room.
In 1971, Marvin Gaye sang to his mother.
In 2019, I talked to my mother's ashes.
Both mothers cried because black boys became black men.
The music stopped when the record did.

Upstate, New York

for James Wright

In Saratoga Springs New York,
there is light before six a.m.
No overcast sky.
And enough visibility to see all before me.
Curious trees witness the rearing of children.
Humble grass that the children of children run
across because the law of make believe requires it.
Monarch butterflies flap their wings—black and yellow,
yellow and black—in harmony.
Traffic logs out.
Morning dew softens my skin.
Small, quiet drops of water forms a kinship with my blackness.
I hate what racism does to me.

Toni Morrison: In Airplane Mode

I stood in an airport when I heard of your passing.
In Albany, heading to Philadelphia.
It was correct I took to the air,
like you did many times before.
The last summer you read a book,
words no longer functioned the way you needed them to.
To create and have nothing else to prove.
A little girl from Ohio.
You listened to the stories of black people.
The small, selected group of black intellectuals shaped American letters.
I placed my phone in airplane mode.
All to ponder were the clouds, the clean blue sky, and plot development.
When black people take to the air,
such amazement and wonder is there.
For a time, to reside above the same clouds
that view gentrification, compromised drinking water, and police shootings.
While practicing literature,
you were preparing yourself
for the moment you would become a shooting star.
Bright, small, present.
Racing across the perpetual night.
When the plane moved through the clouds the aircraft shook.
The moments of turbulence reflected,
the careful diction you selected.
On August 6, 2019, I wanted to wrap you in a blanket of didactic phrases.
That queer language that converts the abstract into the concrete.
You are better off with the angels.
They will not ask for interpretations.
You are better off with eternity.
Time sought to limit you.

Black Lives in an Apple Orchard

Red apples are above us.
Crimson but we do not think of blood.
First fruits kiss the sunrise
(or maybe the sunrise kisses the first fruits)
in an orchard, in the morning.
Rust-bathed trucks stand still.
The men have left them
telling people holding an apple nearby,
that's a good one.
The Tennessee apple orchard
was a former plantation and we are black.
With our arms locked (my wife),
no one doubts that we are together.
When we step in unison,
no one shares their disbelief.
We stand where Adam and Eve
could have stood, and like the first couple,
we are banished. The apples in front of us
remain there.

Meditation: When Dreams Lose Their Grandeur

"There is a connection with us."

Mother-in-Law

She comes from clouds,
white substances I cannot touch.
If I look at her any closer,
I will see where her daughter's smile originates.
Her namesake sleeps in the bedroom with me.
The times she rolls over
she grabs my arm
as taking me to her world of slumber.
I do not tell her mother of the details.
Short hair in the summer,
long hair when autumn arrives,
same pearl necklace her grandmother wore,
my mother-in-law looks at me.
She looks at me when I open the door for her child.
In prayers unheard,
perhaps she asks the saints
to grant me wisdom.

A Nursing Home in Knoxville, Tennessee

The nurse warned the couple of the last fifteen minutes.
One of them clapped off beat while the children sang.
The daughter was thankful for the stars
her lineage painted on her ceiling.
The young mother watched her
slip back and forth between the lands.
The only child heard the abbreviation of her Christian name
and it was Easter again. She ran among the hills
looking for eggs. Underneath the mother's watchful eyes
she learned the difference between boys and men.
Her mother called her father an astronaut after his death.
She sat with her mother—in a nursing home—thinking
about the last Good Housekeeping issue.
She gave up on conversation before
her mother placed her hand
on her wrist and guessed:
I don't belong here, Beth.

When Dreams Lose Their Grandeur

The phrase,
when you are older,
pierces your soul
but you do not know why.

Be aware of the broken glass
because you will see your family—
the ones you will only see
in black and white: the grandfather
who marched in Korea, fighting
in the rich men's war, and the ones
who struggle in your presence
(sometimes you cannot count
on the water pump to work).

When I tell you, I'll see you
next weekend, and I do not show up,
ancient tears surface because you think
all I had to do was buy a new car.

Catch as many dragonflies as you can.
Release them from a jar,
and draw their nugatory wings
on bright, white paper.
I will exhibit your paintings
on my insipid refrigerator door
in my small apartment
when you forgive me,
and let me eat dinner with you again.

Mother's Hour

I'm sure my mother became a saint
after her heart ceased to beat,
when she no longer celebrated
the rainbow after an autumn rain.
Alone on her bed, she saw
the light from the great beyond
and had enough health
to sprint towards it.
In the seconds,
when choices cannot be made twice,
I consult her memory.
I summon the voice
for which I cannot remember its timbre,
and wait for signs and wonders.
I seek for knowledge
from a woman that moved
like a statue when I last saw her.
Like an icon—I touched her feet—
and asked her to pray for me.
It was the first time in years
in which she listened.

I Want You Back

The night Michael Jackson died
you emailed me. The quiet digital
letter possessed all caps.
You were my mother, revealing
a childhood, telling me nothing
mattered more than family.
Five men danced on a stage.
Five black men who did not raise
their hands to strike you. Conversations
became hard for us. When you looked at me
you saw my father, wearing an orange jumpsuit.
He created a debt to the state of Tennessee,
and years of his life served as recompense.
I play all the Jackson 5 tracks
I can listen to:
their outrageous outfits,
loud basslines,
and nostrils opened wide to recover all the air they could.
When you no longer needed air,
you became air. I was no longer
connected to the earth the same way.
I was reborn.
I want you back.

Parental Rights

I wake with you
even though the miles separate us.
Every week day,
your mother screams,
until Jesus, Joseph, and Mary wake.

Brush your teeth in the bathroom.
Look deeper into the mirror,
and you will see my routine from 1992.

On the first day of school,
there are new shoes on your feet.
The night before Christmas,
presents wrapped with care—
are there—
for you to open when we give thanks
for the birth of Christ.

When the humming fridge lacks humanity,
I remember telling you drinking coffee turns you black
(when I last saw you).

In my morning routine,
father, son, and daughters
are under the same roof.

Honor Thy Father

He works twelve hours a day
lifting steel—
checking glass—
building an empire.
Lunch is a pack of crackers and tuna.

The light from the television
is the warmth he connects to.
When he walked through Vietnam,
the steel pressed against his chest.
At nights,
he counted the stars
he carried with him from Tennessee.

The son knows he should like his father.
Although the two do not speak,
he honors the distant parent
like he honors the moon
that is out of his touch.

He works twelve hours,
lifting steel, checking glass,
remembering what he ought to forget.

Long Term Memory

Nanny stands in the front yard.
Sunday dress falling off her body.
Sitting in the living room later,
she looks out the window
and calls me Clarence.

Al Smith, the committed wet, lost
against Hoover. Nanny's mother voted.
She touched history like a farmer touches
his seeds. Clarence lied about eating
a slice of cake before dinner.
Nanny, her father's daughter, marched
outside to find a switch which would not hurt.
She took the lashes while her brother wept
in a corner. In 1941, Clarence flew toy planes
in the backyard. Foreign aggression in Korea
took him from Knoxville, Tennessee. Nanny stood
in the tall grass. Clarence drove away.
Little brother hailed Mary before his plane
crashed in the Pacific Ocean.

Behind the bathroom door
my grandmother washes her mother.
Standing in the hallway I hear laughter.
Nanny splashes water like her daughter once did.
Wrapped in a towel, she is wheeled by,
and refers to me as Clarence, again,
tells me I look better after the war,
and asks me to stay when Johnson calls
for Vietnam.

Driving West

My girlfriend kissed my car's windshield
and told me to hurry back for coffee, lemon pie, and her.
In 955 miles, I will see my mother again.
She is cold, quiet, front yard fence still.
Between Crossville, Nashville, and Jackson
my car leaked oil. Leaving the east on purpose
felt rebellious. Mother made the same trip, too.
Trails of shattered glass followed her.
So did the bad names and poor choices.
Every Saturday night, she darted out of my grandmother's
home like she was a teenager while I read myself to sleep.
After Memphis, the traces of red lips had vanished.
I watched the hours of asphalt travel beneath my car,
behind damp, dark lenses.

In the Morning, He'll Be in Costa Rica

and the ink used to wish him well dries on a birthday card.
He wants a land where I'm not his father.
He grows into being his own man, I cannot bother.

With enough time, he compares the landscape before him.
In East Tennessee, the mountains possess smoke.
In Central America, earth's surface talks to the clouds.
Our hearts beat the same when we see something new.
Our voices are closer than we thought they would be.

For his 18th birthday my son travels, and his birthday card ages.

Passing Grandmother

God gives her three names.
Adam names the animals and the flowers,
but the Lord crafts her identity.
He keeps the knowledge to himself.
When at first sun,
she points to the sky,
(blue, piercing, clean).
She runs after the butterflies in 1941.
Her heart breaks and mends.
The nights she does not listen to her mother,
the man's laughter becomes all in all.
After the first of two babies,
her dialogue to heaven becomes a stream of curse words.
There are days being black creates context for responses.
The babies become children become adults become decision makers.
The bail bonds man does not accept partial payments.
She is too young to be a grandmother.
Her daughter's child asks,
Why is the sky blue?
So God can talk to you.
In cold rooms,
dark hallways,
she does not know who named God
(supreme being does not answer questions).
In a bedroom,
in a small room (with white walls),
she does not believe life flashes before eyes when death is pending.
She prefers to listen to singing birds like she did in 1945.
Outside the grass grows and she takes her three names with her.

Pep Rally for a Daughter

All the songs she listens to
wake her in the morning.

Before the light of the sun is visible,
the ridiculous car pools,
and political locker assignments,
she thinks about my PT Cruiser's cracked windshield,
and the compact discs
I played on Sunday afternoons.

Her classmates do not stand still
and cheer her on as she walks down hallways.

Musicals are magical.
High school is mandatory.

And this child (signs and wonders)
wants the day to slow down.

She knows the difference between
responsibility and irresponsibility
are the questions she asks.

I do not worry about mob mentality with her.
She walks to her own beat.

www.ingramcontent.com/pod-product-compliance
Lightning Source LLC
LaVergne TN
LVHW041301080426
835510LV00009B/822